*Design* David West Children's Book Design
*Illustrations* George Thompson
*Picture Research* Cee Weston-Baker

*First published in Great Britain in 1989 by*
Franklin Watts Ltd, 96 Leonard Street, London EC2A 4RH

© Aladdin Books Ltd 1989

*Designed and produced by*
Aladdin Books Ltd, 70 Old Compton Street, London W1V 5PA

ISBN 0 7496 0086 1

A CIP catalogue record of this book is available from the British Library.

Printed in Belgium

## Contents
| | |
|---|---|
| The nest | 2 |
| Out of the egg | 4 |
| A new world | 6 |
| First swim | 8 |
| The duck family | 10 |
| Eating | 12 |
| Learning to fly | 14 |
| Fine feathers | 16 |
| Ducktalk | 18 |
| Taking off | 20 |
| Duckling facts | 22 |
| Index | 24 |

# BABY ANIMALS

# Ducklings

### Kate Petty

**Franklin Watts**
London · New York · Toronto · Sydney

# The nest

The mother duck searches for a safe and secret place to lay her eggs. She builds a nest with leaves and grass and lines it with her own downy breast feathers. She lays the first egg exactly four weeks after mating. Each day for the next eight days or so she lays another egg. Then she settles down to keep them warm for a month.

**This mother duck is a Widgeon.**

Duck eggs in the nest ▷

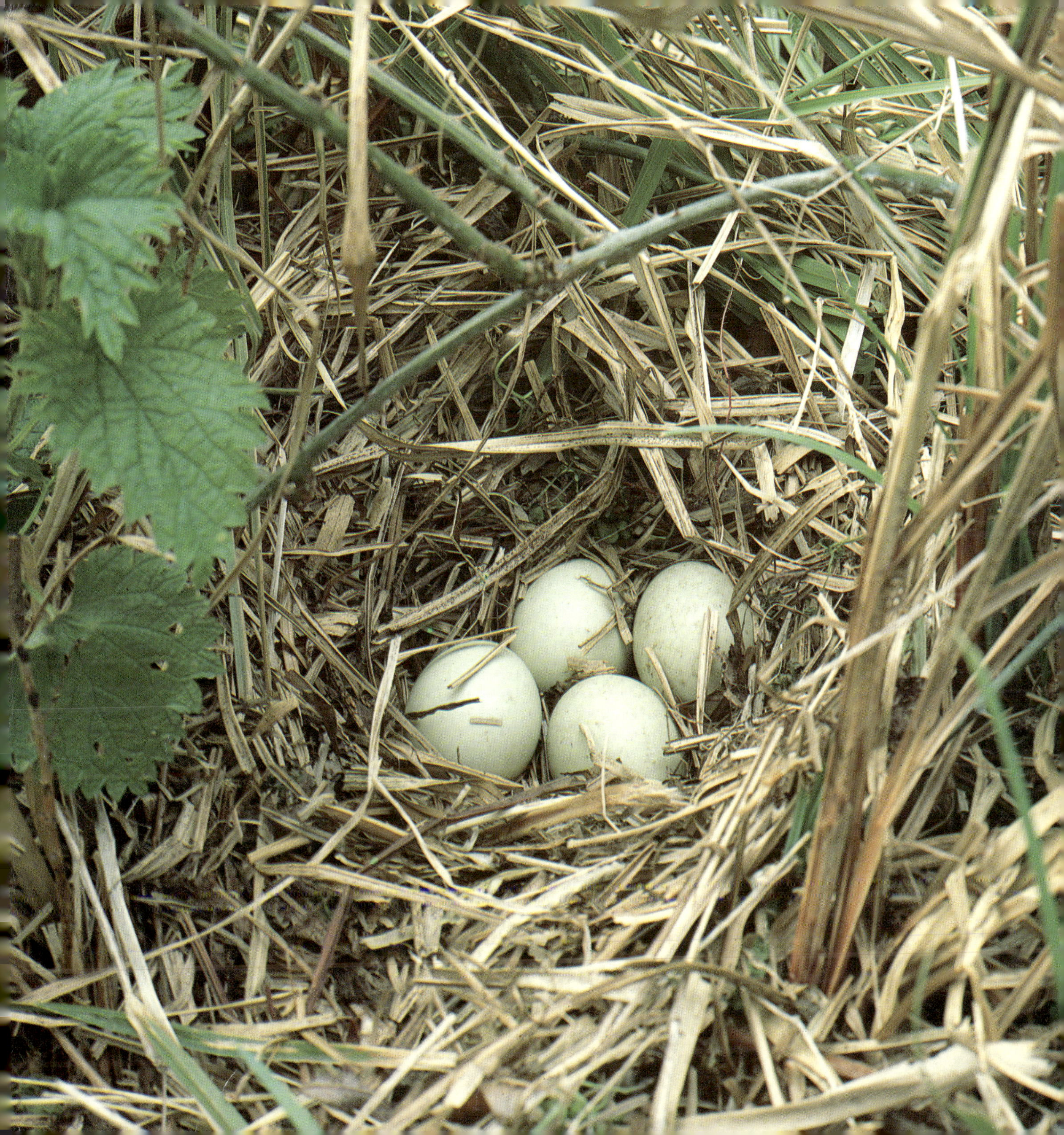

# Out of the egg

A month after the eggs were laid the ducklings are ready to chip their way out. This is hard work for a tiny duckling and it takes several hours. The duckling saws around the shell with its beak and pushes the two halves apart. Then it has to kick itself free. The newly hatched duckling is wet all over and rather trembly after its efforts.

**Inside the eggs the ducklings are chipping at the shell.**

The duckling's head emerges first. ▷

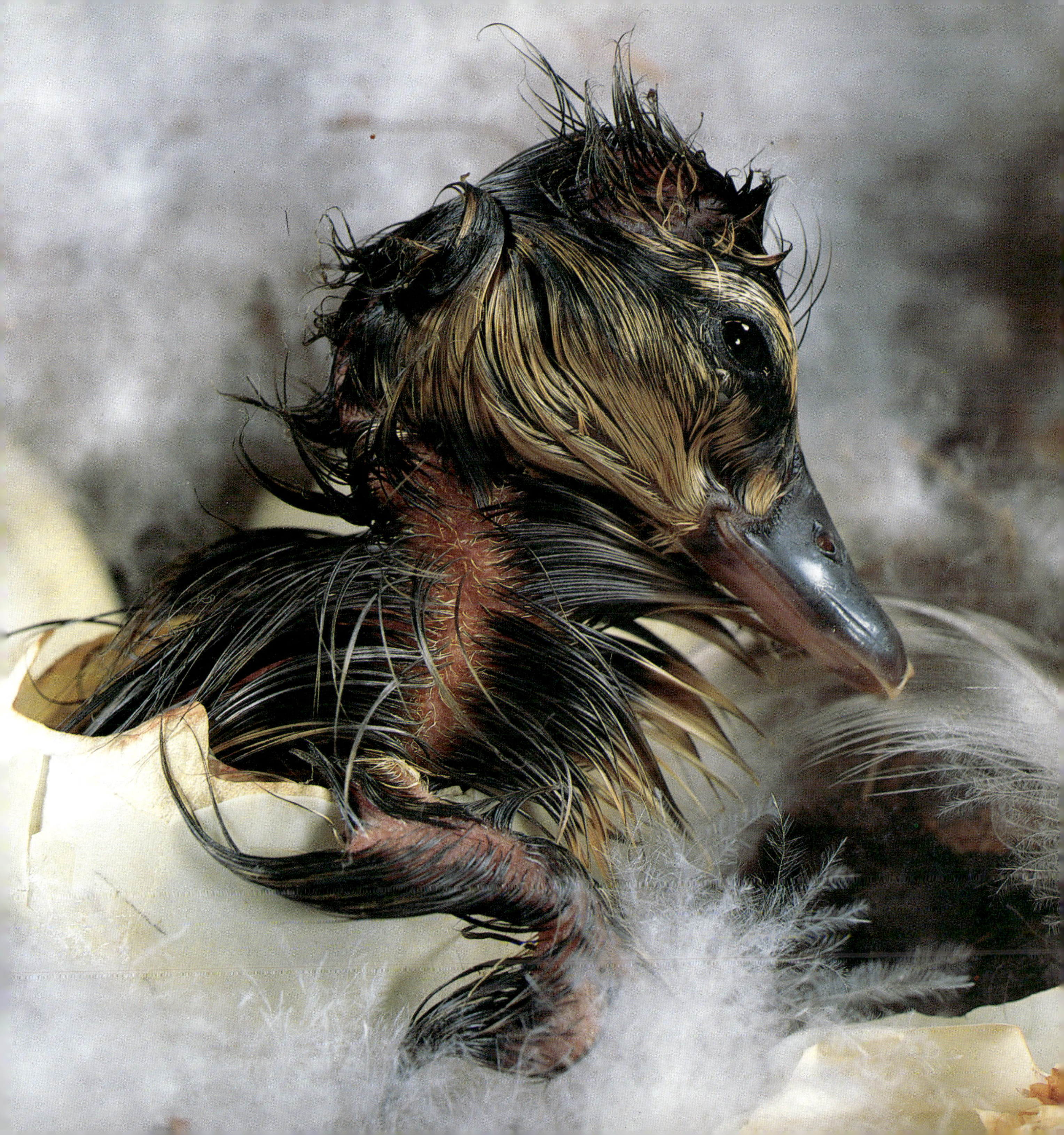

# A new world

Soon all the ducklings have hatched. The mother duck helps to clear away each bit of shell. As their feathers dry out the ducklings start to look very fluffy and sweet, with shining eyes and big, flappy webbed feet. Inside the eggs the ducklings lived off the nutritious egg yolk. Now they are ready to find their first meal for themselves.

**A Mallard duckling finally frees itself from the shell.**

Day-old Mallards ▷

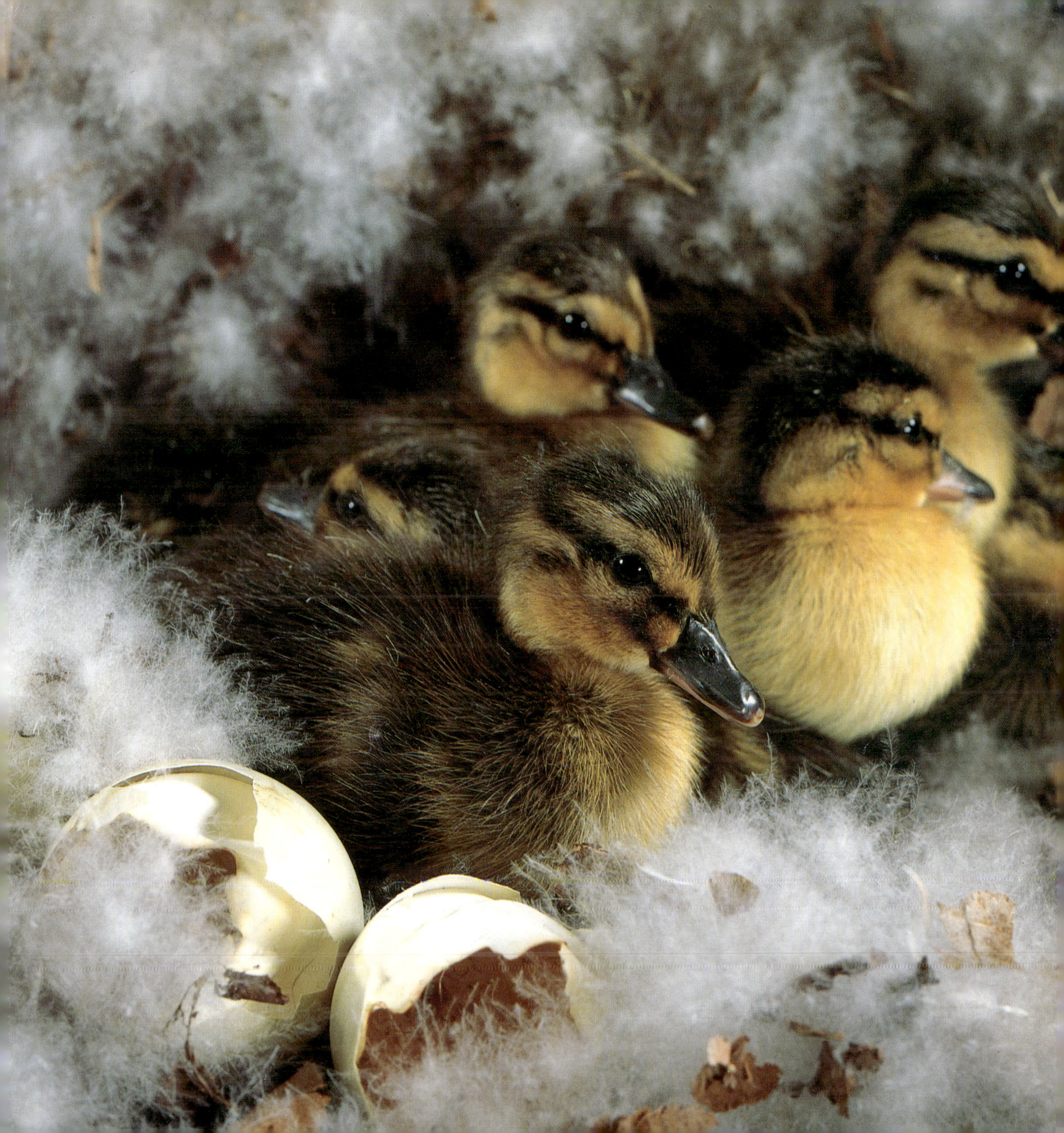

# First swim

Ducklings naturally follow the first creature they see. So when their mother gently pushes them out of the nest and heads for the water, they have no choice but to follow her. Walking is difficult for them at first, but paddling along at their mother's side is really quite easy. Once back on the bank they shake the water from their feathers so they don't get cold.

**The ducklings take to the water without any trouble.**

A duckling dries off after its swim. ▷

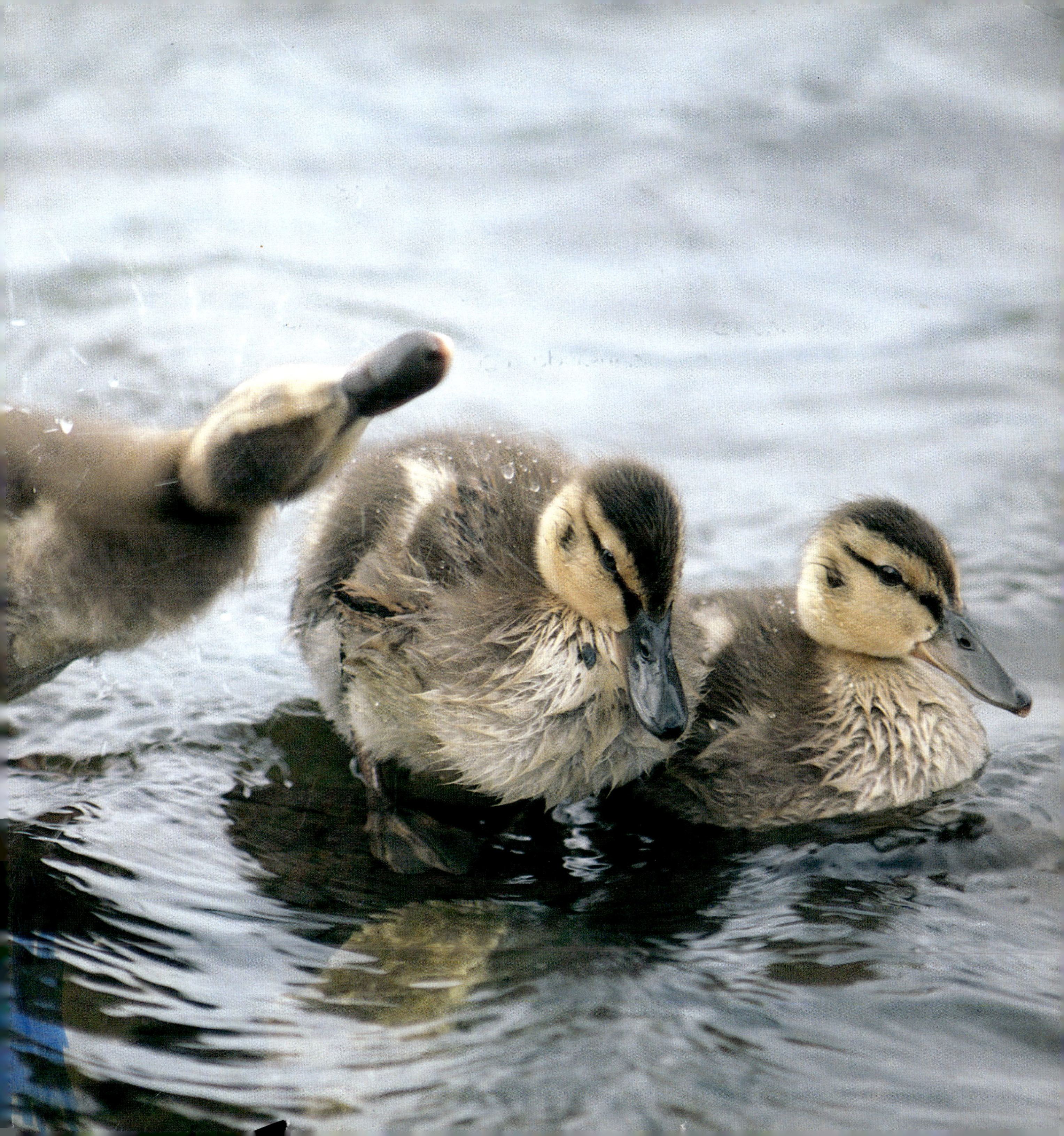

# The duck family

Although the mother duck spent several months with the drake before her eggs hatched, she brings the ducklings up on her own. She keeps them warm in the nest and stays close when they are out of it. They follow her about in a long line and she does her best to protect them from the jaws of hungry predators.

**These are Barrow's Goldeneye ducks.**

Ducklings stay close to their mother. ▷

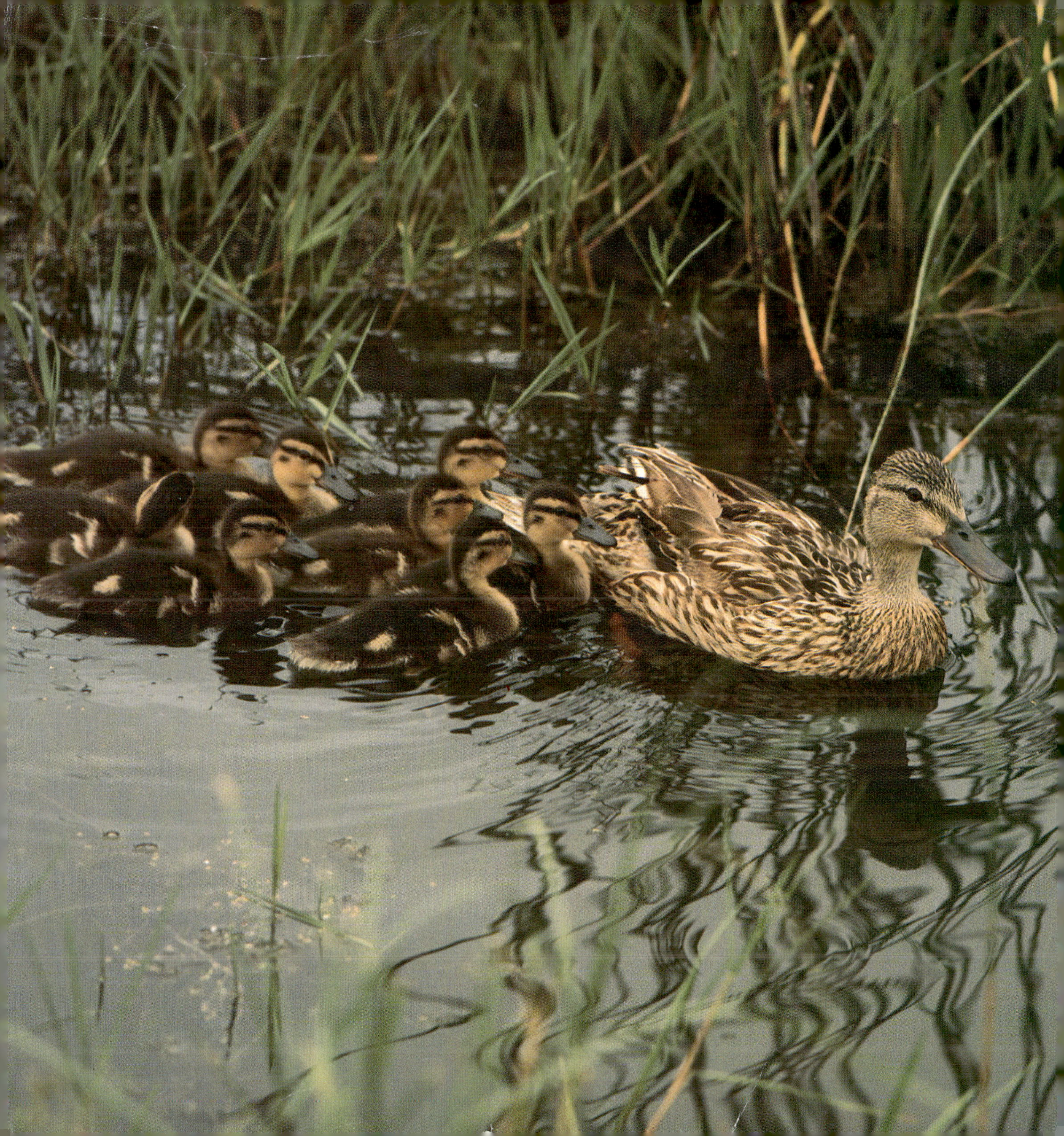

# Eating

Ducklings have to feed themselves as soon as they hatch. They copy their mother as she snaps at little insects hovering close to the water. As they grow older they learn to up-end themselves and dive for creatures below the surface. They eat waterweed too. At night ducks go on land and find berries, seeds and worms to eat, as other birds do.

**It takes time for ducklings to learn how to dive.**

Ducks feeding on land ▷

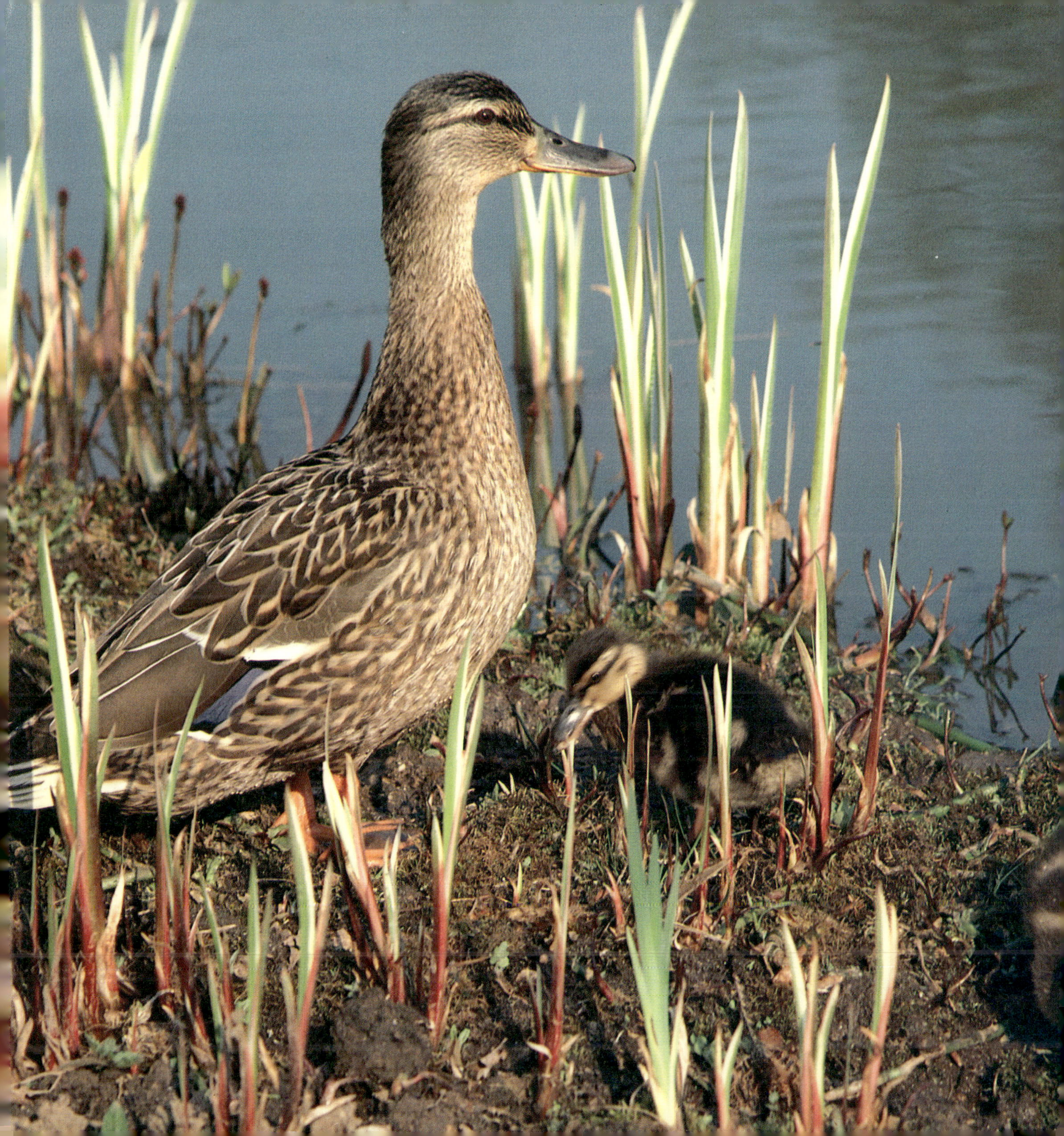

# Learning to fly

The little ducklings cannot learn to fly until their feathers grow longer and their wing muscles strengthen. At first, they just hop into the air and float to the ground. They have to learn to take off by flapping their wings strongly. Once the ducklings can fly the mother no longer needs to protect them.

**These are Spectacled Eider.**

Ducks can take off and land in water. ▷

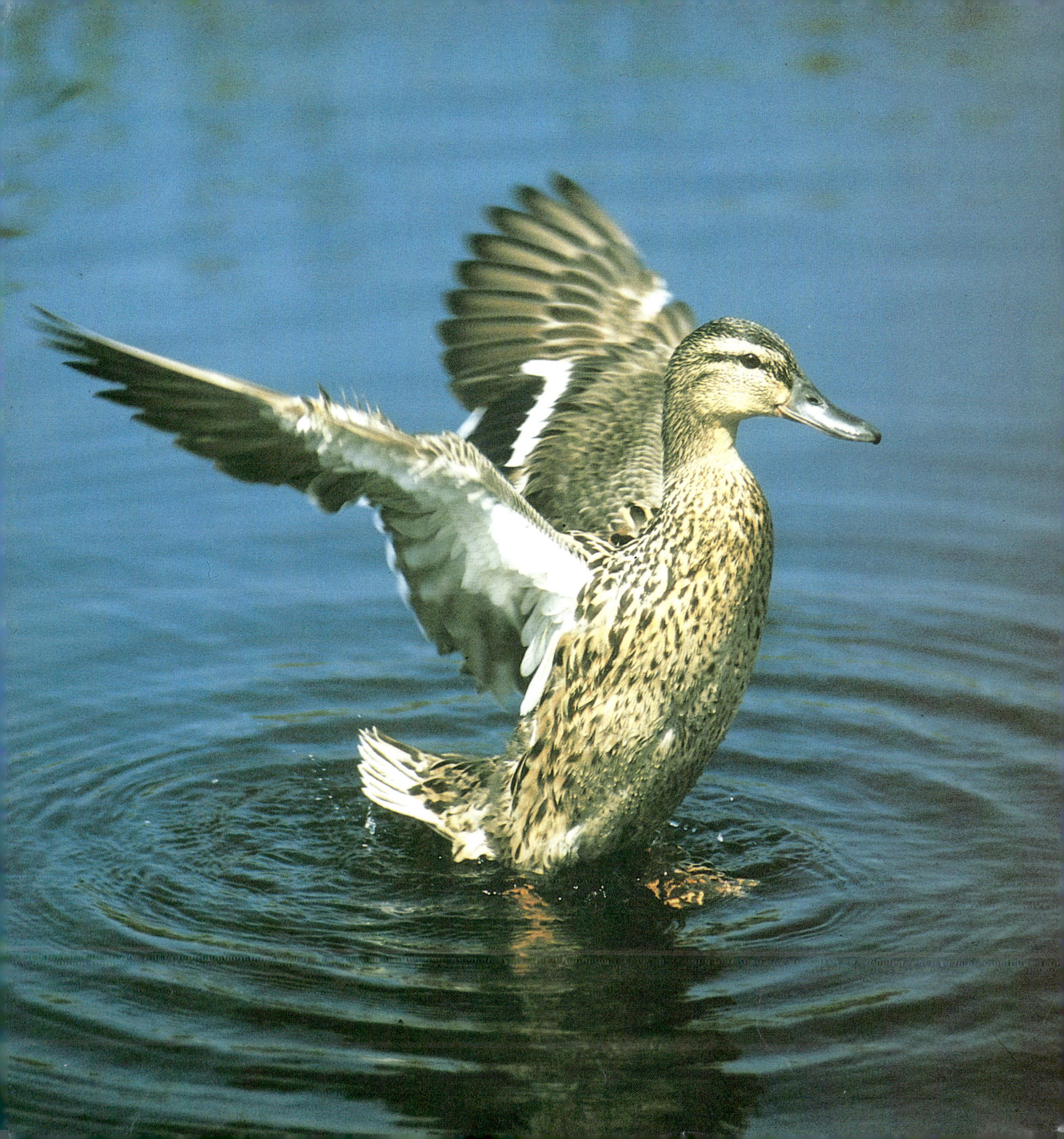

# Fine feathers

Ducklings have to learn to look after their feathers. Feathers keep them warm and dry in wet and cold weather. A duck cleans its feathers by combing through them with its bill. It makes them waterproof by spreading oil over them from the "preen gland" near its tail. Drakes have more brightly coloured feathers than their sisters.

**Male and female Tufted Ducks**

Duckling preening ▷

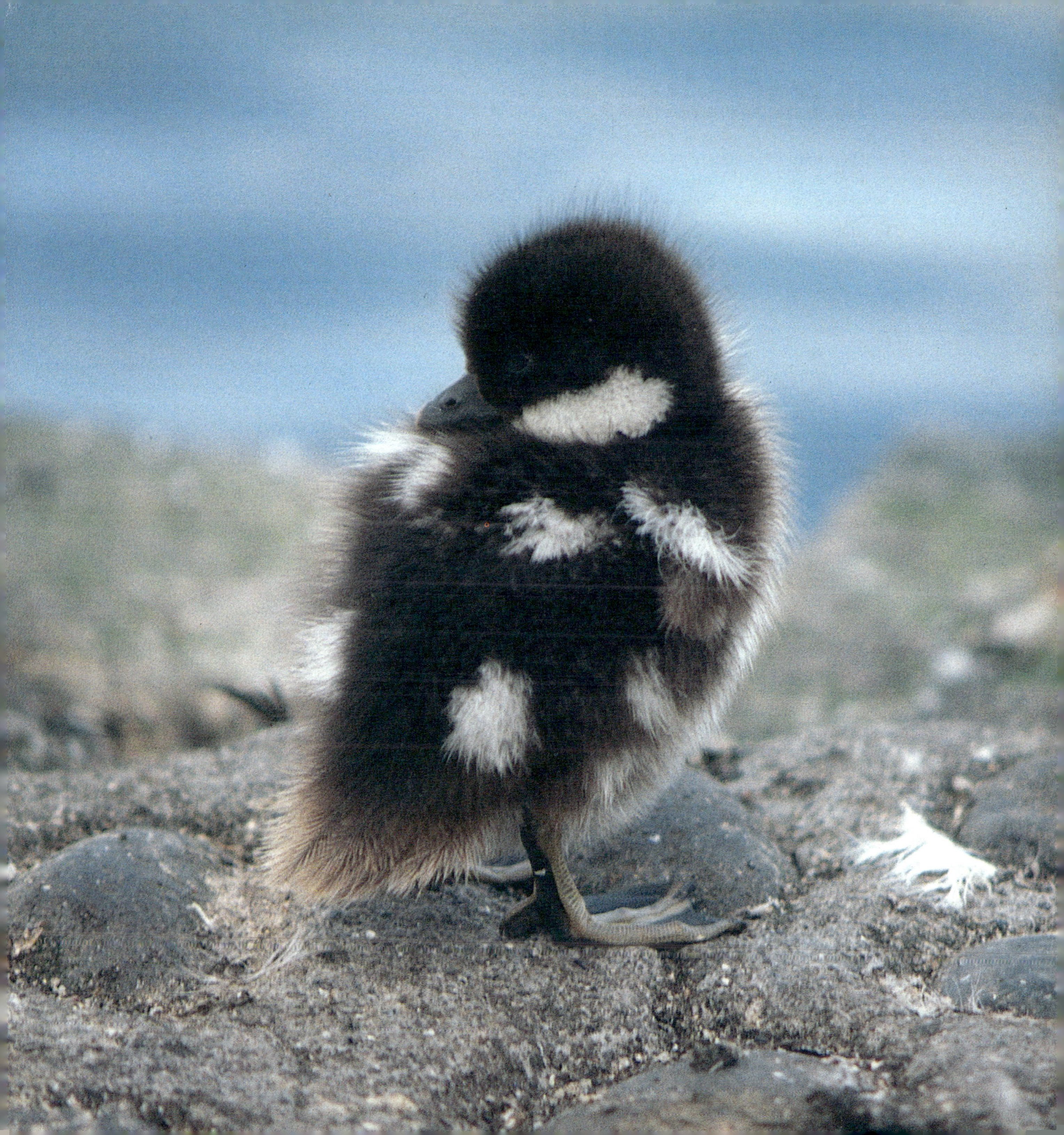

# Ducktalk

By the autumn the ducklings are old enough to choose a mate for the following spring. The young ducks and drakes show off to each other. The female stretches out her neck along the water and nods her head to show that she wants to find a mate. The drake pretends to preen and makes rattling noises. Or he shakes water all about with a grunting, whistling sound.

A Pochard drake showing off to the duck.

The female nods to the drake she has chosen. ▷

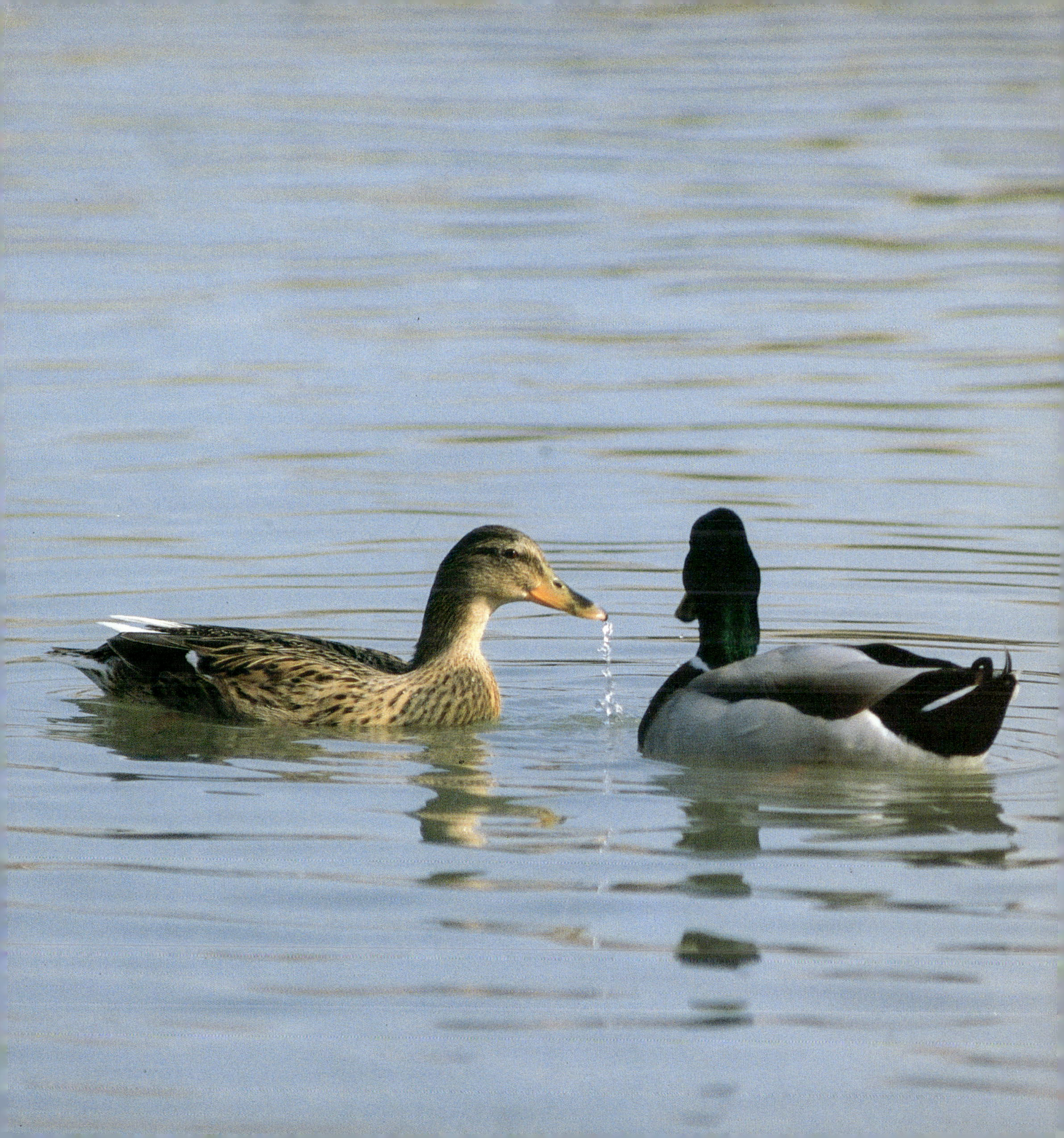

# Taking off

As the weather grows colder the ducks get ready to fly to warmer places where they will find more food. The flock sets off in the evening and flies all night. They rest in the day and then fly on again until they arrive at a suitable place. After the winter many of the ducks return to where they were hatched to raise their own families.

**A flock of Lesser Scaup**

**Ruddy Shelduck flying in a V formation** ▷

# Duckling facts

There are many different sorts of ducks you might see in parks, on ponds or in wild places. Most ducks choose a partner in the autumn and mate in the following spring. The young ducklings hatch two months later. All breeds are full grown by the time they are one year old. Some, like Mallards, are grown up and ready to choose a mate at six months.

**Newborn**

**Adult female**

**Adult male**

# Index

**B**
Barrow's Goldeneye 10
beak 4, 16

**C**
courtship 18

**D**
diving 12
drake 10, 16, 17, 18, 19

**E**
eggs 2, 3, 4

**F**
feathers 2, 6, 8, 14, 16
feeding 12
feet 6
flock 20
flying 14

**H**
hatching 4, 6

**L**
Lesser Scaup 20

**M**
migration 20
mother 2, 6, 8, 10

**N**
nest 2, 8, 10
nodding 18, 19

**P**
paddling 8
Pochard 18
preening 16, 18
protection 10

**R**
Ruddy Shelduck 20

**S**
shell 4, 6
Spectacled Eider 14

**T**
taking off 14
Tufted Duck 16

**W**
walking 8
Widgeon 2
wings 14

**Y**
yolk 6

Photographic credits:
Cover and pages 13, 17 and 21: Ardea; pages 3, 9, 15 and 19: Frank Lane Agency; pages 5 and 7: Jane Burton / Bruce Coleman Ltd; page 11: Udo Hirsch / Bruce Coleman Ltd.